the Persistence of Yellow

"a book of recipes for life."

Written by

Monique Duval

Illustrated by

Joanna Abbott Moss

Acknowledgements

To electric energy man, Kobi, whose instincts and insight come straight from the brightest, yellowest place in the sky amazing everyone who knows him; to my mother, Yolanda, who keeps clapping long after it's proper; to the love of my life, Gerko, who thinks I'm a goddess and please nobody spill the beans; to my absolutely favorite poet and mentor, Naomi—let's meet at Milagritos for a *papa con huevo!*

With special thanks to

Beverly Abbott, Jay Baird, Justi Baumgardt, Beth Bingham, Cate Bradshaw, Doug Cruickshank, Jim Darragh, Josie and Rob Estes, Dawn Ewing, Sonya Groppenbacher, Rachel Harper, Jennifer Hurwitz, Tom Jeffrey, Beth Keane, Liam Lavery, Evan Moss, Donna, Owen & Rebecca Moss, Teri O'Brien, Mary & Koo Koo Pigman, Janet Potter & Family, Diane Roger, Jayne Simmons, Robert & Val Yamada, Tote Yamada, Anne Zadra, August & Arline Zadra and Dan Zadra.

Credits

Written by Monique Duval

Illustrated by Joanna Abbott Moss

Edited by Kobi Yamada

Layout by Steve Potter

ISBN: 1-888387-38-6

Printed in Hong Kong

To my grandmother, my abuelita, my angel...

My dear reader,

    I invite you into this book in the same way my grandmother, my *abuelita,* laughingly invited me into her bright yellow kitchen, her flour-covered hands waving me towards a seat at the head of the table with a story already in progress. While she kept me busy kneading dough, or grinding spices in a *molcajete* or stirring a simmering broth, she told me stories in a strangely beautiful mixture of Spanish and English. Every outrageous question I asked was elaborately answered and decorated like a birthday cake. Sometimes I think she'd invent words if the story called for it. She told me about islands where women had wings. About the art of reading clouds. About the way music speaks to flowers. About how flowers listen. About how everything—even toasters and rolling pins—had a language of it's own. I believed every word with an intense faith that what I was hearing was as true as the bones in the soup. And if I was shaking my head in disbelief—oh, grandma!—then there would invariably appear some form of proof, some synchronous event, that came mysteriously on time—a knock at the door, a tele-phone call, a sudden breeze through the window—something that always gave my faith a place to sit back down. Her words clapped hands with life and danced and sang and prayed and joined with the *rapap rapap* sound of chopping and the *sss* of *masa* on a hot griddle and the *ah ha!* of serendipity. The pulse of words and sounds and smells of that bright yellow place—yellow as saffron, yellow as the curl inside a Marigold petal—seeped into my body through all my senses and became a living part of me.

The Persistence of Yellow is a book about a place like this that exists in all our hearts. No matter who your grandmother was, or what your childhood was like, or what kind of job you have. It's a place where we can stand on a chair on our tiptoes, watching out the window for an angel with unabashed enthusiasm. Consider it a recipe book for the soul. And like a recipe book, it's just a guide, a tool to help you find that place where everything is connected to everything else: faith and action, heart and soul, mind and body. A place where endless possibilities and invention and inspiration and serendipity are all hovering around us offering the right ingredients for our lives. We're all connected and our stories are connected. That's probably why this book landed in your hands like some giant mythological butterfly. We all hope you enjoy yourself as you create your own creations. And don't forget to share your recipes with others.

And now, in the spirit of the moment, I'm going to do a handstand. Don't look if my skirt flips over. I said don't look.

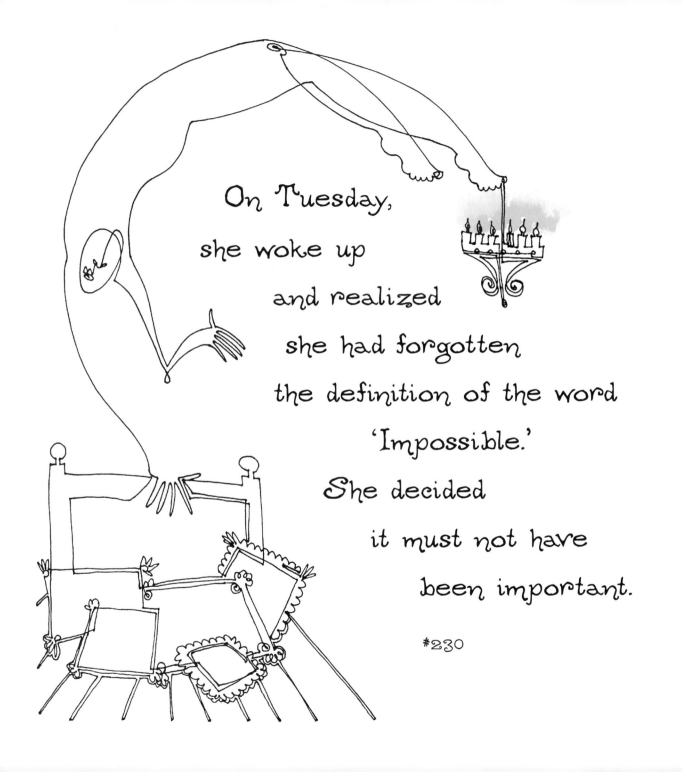

On Tuesday,
she woke up
and realized
she had forgotten
the definition of the word
'Impossible.'
She decided
it must not have
been important.

#230

"Most of my life," she says,
"I've been in search of IT.
And I thought IT came inside
a big box with a bow on top
carefully marked and
labeled and numbered.
I brushed away all the
'incidental' discoveries
like cobwebs.
But now everything counts.
Now I search for traces
of miracles...
and I find them
everywhere."

#172

Today I had a conversation
with my true self. She was
perturbed with me.
She asked me why I had
abandoned her; why I had ignored
all her constant advice.
And then she reminded me of
all the things I had forgotten.
And never once
did she say,
"I told you so."

#188

Despite her
husband's objections,
she gave
a brief demonstration
of her flying technique
to the other ladies
at the dinner party.

#C

I met my dreams
in a dream last night.
They were whining about
the view, the humidity, the
reckless rooms inside my heart.
"We need room for flight,"
they cried. So I'm deconstructing
my tiny house today.
I'm giving my dreams
the starlight as their steeple,
the uncluttered winds
for their kites.

#300

Once upon a time,

a girl prayed for true love.

Her prayer was answered.

She learned to

love herself.

#30

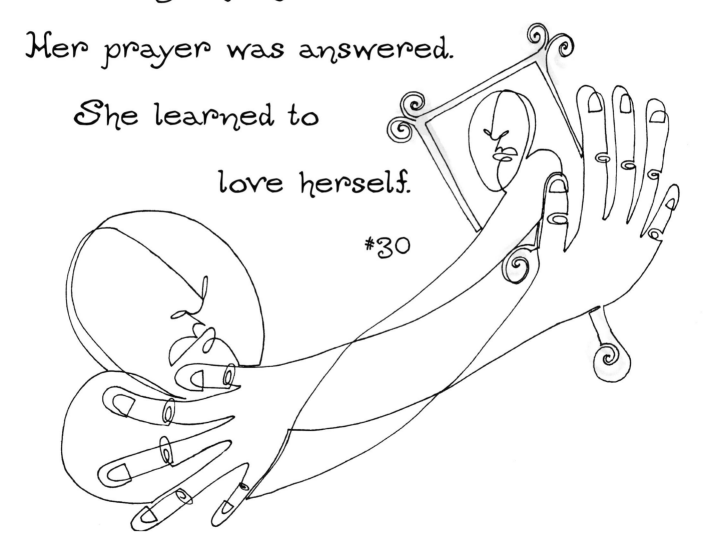

And then quick as light, an angel appeared
and spoke these words into my ear;
"Iscu prula hablinasca ilo. Husca."
Since this is dog language,
and I happen to speak Dog,
I understood it to mean,
"Sometimes,
it is necessary to howl.
No matter who
you wake up."

#146

Once your dreams get so big, they need houses, yellow rooms, empty vases.

#301

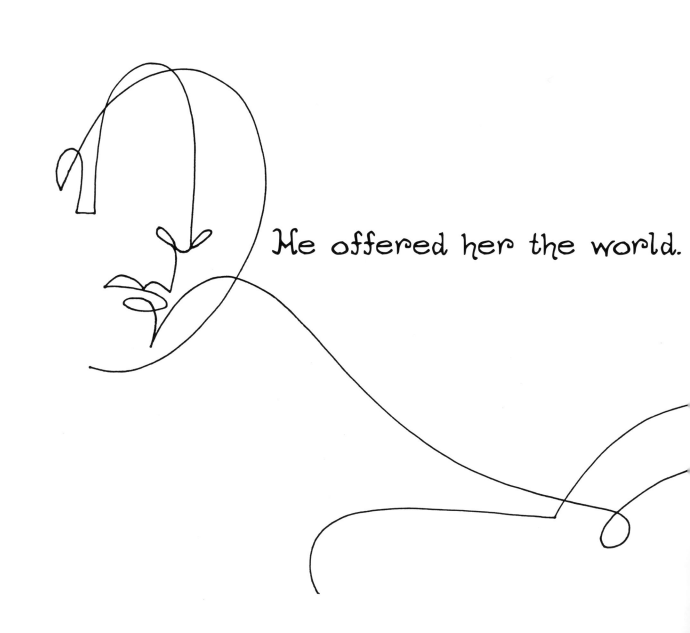

He offered her the world.

She said
she had
her own.

#9

She had a conference with

her angels before breakfast.

Decided how to spend her day:

Climb trees. Run fast.

Sing at the top

of her lungs.

Do the dishes tomorrow.

#41

"And what does
    it feel like?" we asked.
"Well," she said,
        leaning over
        to us like a secret,
    "it feels like a gust
of wind blowing inside
        your heart.
    It feels like
    bright yellow paint."

#81

That's when the rain came down

and we ran—laughing hard, sides hurting—

and there was no shelter for miles.

So we just sat down in the sand

and watched the ocean

swallow the sky.

#122

My dearest,

strolling through a cluster

of century-old trees.

The light here is lovely and thick...

it hangs and billows like webs,

plays tricks upon my eyes and my heart.

If I weren't such a "darn pragmatist"

as you love to call me,

I should think that it is here

where angels live...

#201

She writes a letter. Single-spaced.
Breathless. No pauses. Just lets it
run together and rush like the bottom,
bottom of the waterfall.
She rides her bike to his house.
Takes the long way but pedals fast.
And then she slides those liquid words
under his door. Into the chaos
of his heart.
#237

She stormed
into his life,
took control
of the right side
of his brain...

#78

One Monday morning,
Juanita danced
the Cha Cha Cha,
her sister Sylvia
learned to play the accordion,
Gloria invented a new language.
They all decided
to be true to themselves.

#64

Four men got together

to drink a few Tecates and discuss

their wives' unseemly behavior.

It seems that Juanita learned to dance the Cha Cha Cha,

Gloria decided to invent a new language,

Sylvia suddenly remembered

she could play the accordion, and Yolanda

smelled the sea 2,000 miles away.

#65

"...plaster, blackest ink, sun-dried tomato bagels,

candlewicks, driftwood, kama sutra honey powder

in the tin with the feather, and oranges."

That is what your grocery list says. Now, granted,

your lists are slightly more interesting than the average list.

However, I would not mind, for once, picking up some

milk and eggs. Maybe butter if you wish to be so daring.

I was thinking that exact thought when I ran into

Jose Gonzalez and HIS list at the store the other day.

Lupe had written on one of those manufactured

"things I gotta do today" pads and it was a lot longer

than my list. Well—and don't blame me because it wasn't

my idea at all—we swapped lists. I shopped for his her and

he shopped for you. As a matter of fact, he's still out there.

Let me tell you, it was really gratifying to get

everything in one place for a change.

Bacon bits, iceberg, O B light flows. I mean,

where does a man find sundried tomato bagels

and kama sutra powder in the tin

with a feather? That's a joke, right?

Anyway, that was him on the phone

and he wants to know if you

would be happy with a twenty

pound sack of quick-dry

plaster or one of those

quart-size cartons...

#175

When you catch an angel,

consider yourself fortunate.

They are extremely quick and crafty.

To the untrained eye

they appear as the everyday objects

with which the modern day woman

surrounds herself... #214

"...and what does it mean,"
I asked, "to follow your heart?"
She laughed and beat on her drum.
"So you want my secret recipe?"
she said. I said yes.
"To follow your heart is as
simple as closing your eyes
and listening to the rhythm
of your soul song.
Once you find the beat
you will always walk in tune..."

#194

"We all have needs and desires,"
Juanita said to Anna
as they painted their houses purple.
"In that case," Anna said,
"can we paint the trim lime-green
with pink flowers along the edges?"
"Just what I was thinking,"
she said.

#135

As she was singing
her own special rendition of
'I Did It My Way,'
an angel appeared to her
and threw finely chopped colored
paper about her head
in celebration.

#86

The First Sunday of the month. This is the day we all get together and do secret beauty things. It's a secret because we don't tell anyone. We pluck, poke and probe. We put on green and black masks and then wash them down the drain. We drink a third glass of wine and scream loud when Valorie yanks the hot wax off our legs.

(Only this time I make Maria do it because Valorie and I got in an argument yesterday and I don't want to give her the pleasure of yanking all my hair out by the roots).

Then we all cram ourselves into the tub, spilling water all over the tile floor. Later, we watch Lupe's buns of steel tape while we lounge around and eat chocolate kisses.

Little bits of aluminum wrappers float like leaves.

#253

Last night at Bingo,
Sylvia won the last prize.
"What am I going to do
with a mermaid?" she asked.
"Learn to swim in the
murkiest water,
reinvent
yourself,"
the mermaid said.

#141

Before I
wrote this
letter,
I removed
everything and put it in a
pile by my writing chair:
The part of me that says
"I'm always right"
is on the very bottom.
The bright purple urge to
yell instead of listen is there too.
And I tossed in the ego, the bad
vibes and that baby blue sweater
you always wanted. So this is my
true self wanting to tell you this...

#18©

There is a quiet
wind voice inside of me.
It's the same voice
inside of you.
Delicate and persevering,
it led us towards each other.
Across desert sand,
traffic noise, solitary sky.
I found your little house
by the sea. And I
never wanted to leave...

#189

Every Friday night,
Lupe and Olga
go out on the town.
They wear strapless
dresses to show
off their tattoos of
La Virgin de
Guadalupe,
they fling their
molcajetes out
the window. They split
a beer at the ice house.
Their grandchildren
wonder what the
neighbors think.

#87

You call and say you're on the verge of something big.
So I rush over to watch. This could be good. I push open
the door. You're sitting on your favorite green chair,
legs crossed. You open your eyes for a moment and
whisper to me that there's tapioca pudding in the fridge.
So I tiptoe over and spoon some into the bowl with
the dancing cats along the edge.
I sink into your couch.
I eat tapioca pudding
and watch your verge
of something big.

It's a family thing.
We get tiny plates the size
of a fist. Like saucers for
espresso cups. We say,
"I only want a dab."
But then we get 17 or 18 dabs,
constantly getting up and
saying, "Just a little more.
It can't hurt." We do that with
relationships, too. We say,
"I just want a dab of this,
a touch of that." And then
we are frustrated because we
are never full enough.

#242

"Listen to the waves," you said.

"What waves?" I asked. We were sitting in

one of those outdoor cafes in a city with

no sea. Lots of traffic and smog.

You had this way of hearing and seeing

things as if from some secret realm.

I think of you often. Well, today—

right in the middle of Central Park,

far away from you—I heard the waves.

And then I knew...

#191

And that song you used to sing to me.
The one about the little pigs and the frog who
live under my bed. You sang until I dreamed.
Yesterday, I sang the song to you.
You remembered the words
and sang along.
We laughed. And
I stayed until
you dreamed.

#156

There's a river nearby that runs diagonally between

houses through a small wooded area

probably keeps going into another state pushing

its way into more suburbs more trees more silence

more traffic calmly making its way towards its

destiny moving beyond calamity beyond serenity

not distinguishing between either because the river's

going to meet something bigger than itself

where it will melt into the source it's moving towards

and at that moment the river will lose its reason to be

a river. It does not care. Its purpose was

only to be a river momentarily. It will soon

be vapor. And the vapor will turn into rain.

And the rain will fall into the river. And it is a

river again. I have endless hope in these cycles.

#310

Once upon a time,
she decided to follow her heart.
She flung off her
pinstriped suit and gave
birth to herself.
A new self.
Her true self...

#184

You ask me how things work.
I think of endless cycles, the hum and
spin of everything. So I tell you this:
hold the pale green stalk up high.
And then run hard so the wind will catch
the wings of the dandelion seeds.
Let them fall like sparks, like stars,
back to the earth. I can tell
you are not satisfied. But really.
That's all there is to it:
The persistence of yellow.

#204

She's grabbing things and throwing
them down. Is she looking for her keys?
Lost again? He slants his eyes and
     peers at her from the top of a book.
Now she's in the kitchen. He hears the
cookie jar open, the crunching of potato
chips, the pop and fizz of a soda can
     all at the same time. How does she
do that? He walks to the window and looks
out into the night. The moon, as he
     suspected, is in a sliver, a cuticle,
right over the lake. Making its way
     towards his kitchen, towards his wife
who's eating everything in sight.
     She's wanting everything, nothing,
     all of it, right now, never.

#241

She sat at her mirror at night swinging her leg. Brushing her hair.
Telling the story about the girls. Never mind he's not listening.
He's reading the paper. He says, "Hmm..." So then she tells him about
how she spends her days at the beach when she and the girls drink
vintage wine straight from the bottle and tell only the truth
about everything they can think of.

Nothing is left out about
the dreams, or the secret
ingredients in Lupe's
tamales, or the secret fantasies.
"We say it until there
is nothing left to say," she says.
"And then we watch the boats
and the mermaids and the dark
space between the blades
of light on the water.
The deep,
deep water."
"Hmm," he says.

#17©

There they go again.

Just storming in without asking

Like they own the place.

Rearranging furniture.

Spit polishing all the

shiny things that have

gone dull.
Piecing together all the
broken parts with wads
of celestial chewing gum and
golden thread. I tell you,
these angels are pesky ones.

#171

Today I saw
the future. She was sitting
in a lawn chair in the center of
the road with a sign that said,
"Don't go this way." She doesn't always take
the direct approach. She might camouflage herself
behind traffic jams, alarm clocks, burnt toast and
deadlines causing the urban observer to believe
she's really not there. But no matter what,
she always leaves a little trail of hope leading to
her infinite arms.

#338

"Can you fix it?"
I asked. "I don't know yet,"
  you say and ask for the
screwdriver. I watch you loosen
    each bolt and carefully remove the glass top of my heart.
    "Hmm," you say. "Don't say it like that. What do you see?"
I suddenly feel like smoking a cigarette even though I don't smoke.
You do not answer me. Instead, you sing. You set an alarm clock
  and it rings. You pour in a drop of W-D 40 because you say
it can't hurt. You plant spider lilies and
    promise that they'll
always come back.
  You tell me to
  be still when
I start to laugh.
    But I can't help it.
    I laugh and laugh.

        #254

And then she stands there and reads it
as if each item were the ingredients
for a sauce..."Yes, yes I know
I asked for an angel.
But does she have to
make those lists of
things for me to do?
She's so Type A.
Couldn't you send
me one who likes
to sip tea and knows
the definition of the word
'demure'?"

#249

They are inseparable. Yesterday, the three of them
decided to have a hot peppermint tea party in the
middle of the lake while sitting in a canoe and
worried that their lives were becoming predictable.

#141

Here is the wall with the
antique paint, cracked plaster
and fat pencil lines marking
each inch towards womanhood.
Here is a page of a secret diary.
The day you dreamed something
impossible, wrote it down anyway
and hid it in the cigar box
with the other collection
of impossibilities.

#161

I know I can be annoying. I give tasks.

Ask anyone. My dog is looking at me.

I can tell she wants something urgently.

She looks like her head is

about to pop off.

That's her "give me what

I want right now" look.

I guess what goes

around comes

around.

#324

I invite you for tea and
swinging on my front porch.
You bring me paper flowers and
bits of poetry. I want to
show off Chata, my brilliant dog.
I say, "Sit girl." So she spins around
and flops upside down for a
belly rub. She has no pride.
You say you have to go.
I watch you walk to the
gate, down the block.
Chata follows you
home. And then
I do too.
Forever.

#216

...and on clear days

she discovered

she could make things float away:

Rubber balls, the neighbor's

chickens, metallic objects were

reported missing.

She wondered if she could

make things come back to her.

She thought about him, summer days.

#63

"What kind of broth is this?"

she asked.

"Life," the old woman said.

"Boil your first kiss

until it is violet like a sky.

After it cools,

stir it until it

turns yellow like the

wings of a butterfly.

Then laugh into the potion to

make more good

than bad.

That is the broth

of life."

#120

Elena puts her hand on
her wide hip and gives a big sigh.
"Where is everything today?"
she asks and looks into a yellow field
where her house used to be,
where her garden used to grow.
"I guess I'll have to
start again." And then
she sat down to invent
a new world, a better one.
One that lasts.

#130

Once a day she tells

the spin to sit still,

the twirl to behave, the laugh to whisper;

the dream to sleep. And for a moment

she was untwirled, whispered

and dreamless...

#333

I beg for
your forgiveness.
Last night I ate the moon.
I was standing there wishing
I could be so close to you
so far away.
Tonight I'll give the moon back.
I'm still hungry for you.

#142

There's a place
inside her heart she
reserves for him.
It has good eastern light,
sea breeze and if you
stand on your toes,
you can see
a thousand miles
away.

#67

"So, where's the key?" I asked.

"What key?" you said. "Oh come on.

Don't tell me you don't have

a way to open this?"

I shook it. I sniffed the crack.

I pressed my eye to the keyhole.

That's when I saw it:

Celestial wings, secret notes,

constant light, a way towards

something familiar. "See anything?"

she asked...

#202

Everything melted,

rained, unraveled,

became, grew wings,

attempted flight,

flopped, tried again,

succeeded.

Just another day.

#317

My daughter asked me
how to fly, never thinking
she could not learn.
She thinks
I have the
recipe
for flight.
So we climb a tree
and watch the evening sky.
And wait for the
necessary ingredients.

#309

I say, "It's all black and white."

I say, "It all adds up." But you, in your
inevitable way, insist that the colors are hidden.
So you scratch the surface and find the azure.
And you say nothing adds up at all.
"Infinity + Infinity is beautiful blue chaos," you say.

#341

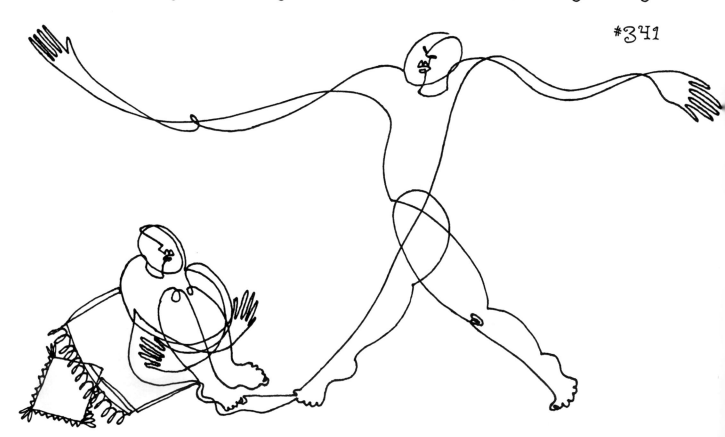

"Once you get over the fear,

then it's a cinch," she said.

And then she leaped

into a mountainous and unexplored

region of her heart.

#115

What do angels look like? I saw one today wearing gaudy jewelry, spoke with a thick Spanish accent, quoted 'Chakespeare.' She said, "All the world's a stage and sometimes you just gotta roll with los punches."

It's a secret. Tiptoe.
Whisper. Hold it inside your
sweaty palm until she comes home.
Then rush over and
open it under her window with
the good eastern light.
And when she smiles, tell her
it's everything. Everything.

#234

I promise you it will be safe here, inside my heart.

I planted it in my windowbox with the Rainbirds,

the Dreamflowers, pinwheels and pogo sticks.

Now, when the wind blows,

my garden clanks and whirs and

sings your name...

#213

And then you sent your angels to
help organize my heart.
They put everything in polite
stacks and piles of "yes" and "go" and
"no" and "extraneously outrageous."
But they put you in a spot all
by yourself floating in the sun and moon
and candle shadows and wrote your
name in bright yellow weatherproof
paint on the walls,
in the walls, through
the walls.

#151

Thousand mile stare.

Endless. With it's own rhythm.

Makes you want to pull off to the
side of the road and sit on the hood
and let that feeling rain back
into the earth.

#233

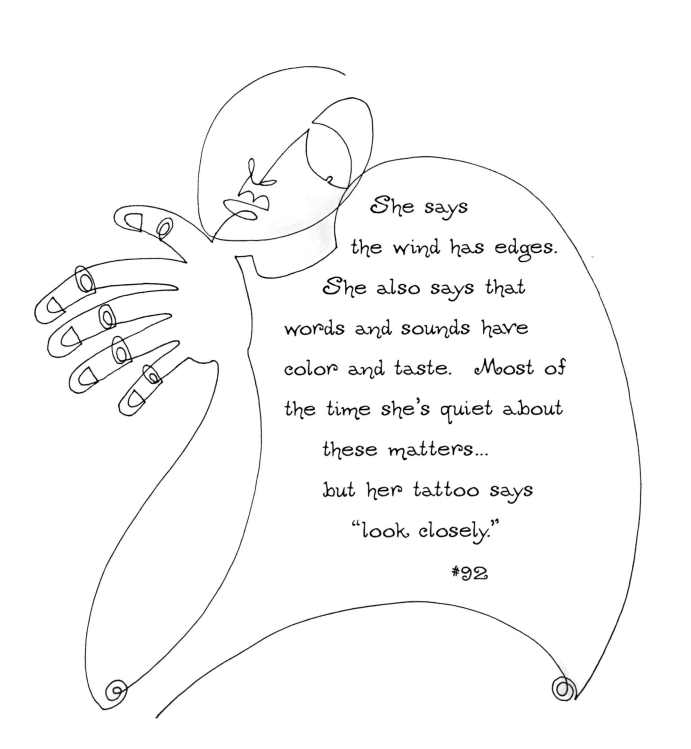

She says
   the wind has edges.
She also says that
words and sounds have
color and taste. Most of
the time she's quiet about
   these matters...
   but her tattoo says
   "look closely."

#92

Cook. Do the dishes. Clean. Cook. Do the dishes. Clean. Cook. Do the dishes. Clean. Read a fashion magazine. And then she realized that her chains were made of nothing but webs and spit and shoe polish, dried-under-the-table chewing gum and stuck-on bits of food. So, she decided that if she must have chains, she would rather be chained to her dreams. Now, she follows obediently where they lead.

#248

And then

your weatherwise heart

foretold of gusty winds and

sodden skies. But you did not know

about my little silver boat...

the one I climb in during storms,

the one that carries me

through and lands me on dry shore,

on mountaintops.

#157

...and those worlds you used to create for me.

Remember? We'd sit on the floor,

Grandma's old quilt draped over our heads.

"Invisible," you'd say. Pure dark space until

we looked up and noticed the pinpricks of

light piercing the fabric.

"Stars," you'd say.

#221

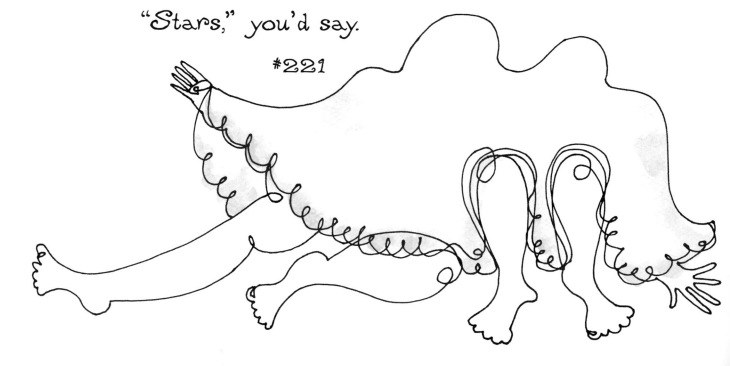

"What shall I do today?"
She thought as she brushed her
hair a thousand times.
  "I will put on the pink dress with the
  tiny white dots. I will dust the furniture and
    teach the cat to fetch..." And just then,
a strange wind pried open her bedroom window
and she suddenly had an uncontrollable urge
  to spin and howl, to jump on her freshly
made bed with her eyes shut tight.
  In other words, she was on the
        brink of a new discovery...

#170

I was sitting alone
minding my own business
as always when that
winged angel showed up again.
She always has some elaborate
advice about pet fur;

or the ozone layer

above my house.

But today she was silent.

She said it was time

I did all the talking.

#302

About the Author

Those of us who are most familiar with Monique Duval's art have always hoped that she would someday write a book, and here it is. Monique is already a legend in the soft-aired streets of her hometown of San Antonio, Texas, where once she strung beads, cut tin and invented a line of wearable jewelry-art that was revered as precious iconography the moment it appeared. Lucky stores, galleries and boutiques placed it right next to the register, knowing it would disappear in a matter of minutes. I sold it when I traveled, like a special agent, hand-to-hand. People I didn't even know approached me, speaking in low, urgent tones, "Do you have any more of those brooches?" Monique always wrote deliciously eccentric and luminous passages of prose to accompany her jewelry-art— and the writers who loved her kept bugging her to MAKE A BOOK!

Her old Texas buddies can't stand it that she moved to Baltimore. Good friend, blunt trickster, little sister, funny neighbor, visionary writer and artist—she is loved and treasured wherever she goes. With a stunning life story, it is impossible to know what she'll do next. Hopefully she will keep putting her voice on pages where more and more people may find it. *The Persistence of Yellow* is a blessing to us all.

Naomi Shihab Nye

About the Illustrator

To someone who knows Joanna Abbott Moss, it comes as no surprise that the first book she has illustrated is titled *The Persistence of Yellow*. Joanna is a lover of sunshine, kindness and the illumination from life's lessons. That she should be teamed up with a writer who obviously shares the same enthusiasm for life's journey is as brilliantly simple as one of her one-line illustrations. While drawing, Joanna never lifts her hand from the paper, allowing a continuous connection between heart, mind, hand, pen and paper until each illustration is complete. During this uninterrupted process, she winds her way through the finest details of elbows and hands, tying together hearts and hints of smiles.

Follow the line of one of these illustrations. See if you can find where it begins and where it ends. In between, you will find Joanna Abbott Moss: a simple mix of child-like innocence and a powerful expression of soul-deep emotion. Enjoy the ride.

To order additional copies of *The Persistence of Yellow*,
or to receive a free catalog of Compendium products,
call or write today:

COM·PEN´·DI·UM™
Incorporated

Publishing and Communications
Edmonds, Washington

*E*nriching the lives of millions, one person at a time.

This book may be ordered directly from the publisher,
but please try your local bookstore first!

Call toll free (800) 91-IDEAS
114 Second Avenue South, Suite 105, Edmonds, WA 98020

www.compendiuminc.com